P9-BIT-275

BUT THERIOUSLY FOLKTH...

by
Johnny Hart

FAWCETT CREST • NEW YORK

B.C.—BUT THERIOUSLY FOLKTH....

A Fawcett Gold Medal Book
Published by Ballantine Books
Copyright © 1975, 1976 Field Enterprises, Inc.
Copyright © 1982 Field Enterprises, Inc.

ISBN 0-449-14488-2

Manufactured in the United States of America

First Ballantine Books Edition: August 1982

10 9 8 7 6 5 4 3 2 1

11·24

11-25

11-27

11-29

12-1

guarantee

a document that expires on the same day as your engine-mounts.

12-2   hart

125

He got arrested once for defacing a crossword puzzle.

WHAT ARE YOU GIVING YOUR KID THIS YEAR?

A 12-POUND BAG OF CONFETTI.

12-8

ISN'T THAT EXPENSIVE?

NOT REALLY...

WE'RE GRINDING UP HIS CHRISTMAS LIST.

12-20

12·23

12.26

1·3

1-5

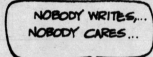

1-7

1-9

1·12

1.13

1.26

1-28

2·2

2·3

2-4

2-5

2.9

3.10

2.11

2-13

2-16

CAUTION
FALLING
WHEEL
ZONE

* See UNITED NATIONS

2-18

LEAP YEAR COMES BUT ONE IN FOUR,

'CAUSE EVERY FOUR, THERE'S ONE DAY MORE,

SO ADD ONE DAY— IT WORKS OUT FINE,

UNLESS YOU'RE BORN ON TWENTY-NINE.

Dear Fat Brood,
I recently found a
pair of panty hose in my
husband's trunk...

ADVICE COLUMN

...should I say something
or just forget it?

Concerned in Toledo

2-21

Dear Concerned,
Unless he's an elephant
... say something!

ADVICE COLUMN

2-24

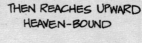

A TREE STARTS OUT
WITHIN THE GROUND,

THEN REACHES UPWARD
HEAVEN-BOUND

...YET NEVER MAKES IT,
QUITE, YOU SEE,

...I FEAR A TREE IS
MUCH LIKE ME.

3-2

3-3

3·4

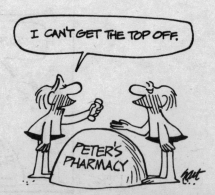

3.9

3-19

3·26

3-30

4-19

4-22

4-24

WHY DO YOU CALL YOURSELF A "REFUSE" COLLECTOR?

PETER'S REFUSE SERVICE

BECAUSE OF COCKTAIL PARTIES.

WHAT'S THAT GOT TO DO WITH IT?

PETER'S REFUSE SERVICE

4-27

CAUSE WHEN I INTRODUCE MYSELF AS A GARBAGE MAN, ALL I GET SERVED ARE THE RINDS.

PETER'S REFUSE SERVICE

5.5

5·13

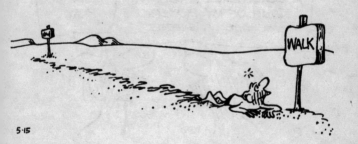

5-15

5-17

5-19

5-20

SUCK

5-21

THANK GOODNESS THE
EARTH IS LUMPY.....

5-22

..OR I'D BE TREADING
DIRT ALL DAY.

ANIMALS CRAVING AFFECTION SHOULD
APPROACH THEIR ADVERSARIES IN
THE SUBMISSIVE POSITION.

5·24

BATTER-UP

WILEY'S DICTIONARY

6·4

the traditional cry of
a desperate baker.

WILEY'S DICTIONARY